6 MINUTE MORNING

stretching

6 MINUTE MORNING

stretching

FAYE ROWE

PaRragon

Bath · New York · Singapore · Hong Kong · Cologne · Delhi · Melbourne

First published by Parragon in 2007

Parragon
Queen Street House
4 Queen Street
Bath BA1 1HE, UK

ISBN: 978-1-4075-1794-0

Printed in China

Created and produced by the Bridgewater Book Company Ltd.
Photography: Ian Parsons
Model: Louisa Jarvis
Exercise consultant: Samantha Fuery at Crysalis Fitness

The views expressed in this book are those of the author but they are general views only and readers are urged to consult a relevant and qualified specialist for individual advice in particular situations. Parragon hereby excludes all liability to the extent permitted by law for any errors or omissions in this book and for any loss, damage or expense (whether direct or indirect) suffered by a third party relying on any information contained in this book.

The Bridgewater Book Company would like to thank JupiterImages Corporation for permission to reproduce copyright material on pages 7 and 9.

Caution
Please check with your doctor/therapist before attempting this workout, particularly if you are suffering from an injury, are pregnant or have just had a baby. It is recommended that new mothers wait at least six weeks post partum before participating in exercise (12 weeks if it was a Caesarean birth). If you feel any pain or discomfort at any point, please stop exercising immediately and seek medical advice.

CONTENTS

INTRODUCTION

If you want to look and feel your best, making time every day to stretch can help you to achieve your goals. Not only will stretching work to counter the muscle-shortening effects of exercise and help you develop toned, lean limbs, but it will also make you more flexible.

Stretch for life

If you've never really put much thought into how stretching can benefit your health and your body, this book will help you realize what an important part of any health and fitness regime it really is. Regular stretching will help to reduce the risk of injury to your joints, muscles and tendons when you do exercise. Plus, it's a great way of relieving any soreness and tension you may feel after a gruelling workout.

Some people find they reach a plateau with exercise, and many health and fitness trainers recommend stretching to help you get the body you really want.

Spending just 6 minutes in the morning doing the stretches in this book will help you to develop the kind of body that makes other people envious. But this plan isn't just supposed to last for two weeks, it's a plan for life. The longer you keep it up, the better you will look and feel.

Stretching develops your muscles in a different way than cardio- or other weight-based exercise does. So, if you already put the time and effort into keeping fit, you should really be dedicating a set amount of time each day to stretching. Plus, it's a great way to stay in shape if sweating it out in a gym simply isn't your thing.

While most forms of exercise will help you to burn calories and fat while strengthening and defining the muscles, stretching helps to tone and lengthen them. The result is that you can appear slimmer, even if you haven't lost any weight. However, if you practise regularly, the toning effects of stretching can make it easier to shift stubborn pounds and give you a more streamlined silhouette overall. So, you'll be one step closer to fitting into your 'skinny' jeans! You may even find that you look taller, because some of the stretches in this book will help you to develop a better posture.

Stretch to relax and detox

If you need any more convincing, you'll be pleased to learn that stretching also has great benefits for the mind. While it does require a degree of concentration, to make sure you're doing each stretch correctly and to the best of your ability, you'll soon realize how relaxing it can be.

Since stretching is best done in silence or to slow and soothing music, it can almost be like meditating. Setting aside just 6 minutes in the morning for the routine will help to put you in a positive frame of mind for the day to follow. As you become more familiar with the different stretches, you can combine the movements with deep breathing and positive visualizations, which will help you to clear your mind from clutter. Stretching is also a great way to stimulate the lymphatic system, which in turn helps to cleanse your body of toxins and boost circulation. So, if you're in need of a healthy boost, this book is also an ideal way to kick-start a detox diet.

Plus, you don't have to be super-fit to do the stretches. It's the perfect starting point for beginners or people with an existing medical condition, such as asthma, which may make it hard to do more energetic forms of exercise.

The two-week plan

All of the 34 stretches in this book aim to stretch out your major muscle groups. Each section targets a different part of the body and the two-week plan will help you to combine the variety of stretches for maximum results.

Each stretch lasts for approximately 30 seconds and it's easy to see how you can combine different stretches to create a 6-minute routine. It's realistic to hold most of the stretches for three sets of around 10 seconds, with a brief pause between. As long as you do what you feel comfortable with and don't pause for more than a couple of seconds at a time during the routine, you'll be doing enough to make it effective. If you can't always find time to do the routine in the morning, you can do it in the evening before bedtime. The reason that we recommend doing it in the morning is because of the mind- and body-boosting benefits mentioned above. But, as long as you are doing it regularly – ideally every day – then you will see results.

While the two-week plan is a great starting point, you should aim to keep doing the stretches every day – for life! The effects of stretching are cumulative, so if you suddenly stop for any length of time, you will lose more or less all the flexibility you've worked so hard to develop. This is because muscles respond more easily to other forms of exercise, such as running or cycling, which make the muscles contract and shorten. Even everyday walking will have this effect on the muscles, so you can see how essential stretching is to keeping you lithe and limber.

What you will need

You don't need a great deal of equipment to do the stretches in this book, although there are a few things that may be worth purchasing. For starters, you should get your hands on a few good pieces of clothing that are comfortable, breathable and made from a stretchy material so that they won't restrict your movements. Most high-street sports shops offer a good range of sportswear and there are some great ranges designed especially for stretching-based exercise, such as yoga, which would fit the bill.

You may want to buy a padded exercise mat to work on, because it will help to stop you from slipping on the floor, as well as being a comfortable surface for exercise. It's not essential that you wear trainers to do the routine – either bare feet or a comfy pair of non-slip socks will do just fine. Alternatively, you could look into buying a pair of 'yoga shoes', which are halfway between socks and trainers and give your feet some support while helping to stop you from slipping.

Make sure you have an alarm clock or wristwatch to hand to help you time the stretches so you know you are doing them for the correct amount of time. All you need now is a positive frame of mind.

Getting started

A good way to start is to spend a quiet afternoon flicking through this book to help familiarize yourself with the various stretches. The exercises are explained with step-by-step instructions, and are illustrated so you know exactly how to do them and how they should feel. Once you've changed into your comfortable clothes, you should switch off the television or any telephones and put on some soothing music. Designate a space in your home that's large enough for you to extend your arms and legs without knocking anything over and, with the two-week plan to hand, you can begin your routine.

You should always make sure you are warm before you stretch, so take a brisk walk around your home or march on the spot for a few seconds to help get your muscles into gear. You should always do this general warm-up, especially if you've just jumped out of bed in the morning. But, rest assured, there is little risk of pulling any muscles while doing the stretches, as long as you stick with what you're comfortable doing.

One golden rule to consider while stretching is that you should try to do each one to the best of your ability, but you should never push yourself so far that you feel pain. All the stretches require you to hold them for a maximum of three sets of 10 seconds. It can be tempting to 'bounce' while in the stretch to try to get down even further, if you are reaching for the floor, for example. However, this can strain the muscles, so you should avoid this.

If, once you've got used to stretching, you feel that you could improve your performance, you can try to increase the stretch by slowly and gently moving further into position. If you ever develop a persistent pain as a result of doing the stretches, make sure you see your GP for advice.

It sounds silly, but you must remember to breathe at all times. Many people have a tendency to hold their breath as they hold certain poses, which isn't advisable. Make sure you breathe deeply and slowly throughout the routine, because it will help deliver oxygen to the muscles and make the stretches more effective.

Don't give up!

Exercise is easy to let slip when you're feeling under the weather, and it's fine to give your body a break every now and then. But, if you ever feel like you want to give up, read these top motivational tips:

• Visualize how you will look and feel if you stick to the programme rather than letting it slip. It should be enough to spur you on.

• Remember that waking up 6 minutes earlier will not encroach massively on your sleeping time. You'll feel much more alert for doing the stretches than you would for having the extra time in bed.

• Not only is stretching good for your body but it's good for your mind, too. So, even if you're feeling down, it's the perfect thing to do!

Seated hamstring stretch

The hamstrings are the muscles running up the backs of the thighs to your bottom. It's common for people to suffer with tight hamstrings, especially if they do a lot of sport, which is why it's great to stretch them out. If you don't stretch, tight hamstrings can cause the hips and pelvis to rotate backwards, resulting in bad posture.

1 Sit down on the floor with your legs straight out in front of you, keeping your feet flexed. Sit up straight so your back isn't hunched and place your hands on your hips.

2 Lean forwards from the hips, letting your upper body drop down towards your feet. You can extend your arms and try to touch your toes, although if you do this, make sure that you don't curve your back.

3 Hold for 10 seconds but don't bounce. Return to the starting position and repeat twice more.

WATCH POINT
This stretch works both hamstrings at the same time so you get double the benefit!

1

2

Inner thigh stretch

This stretch targets the muscles in the inner thighs, which are called the adductors. It's an easy way to stretch both the legs at once and is great if you combine it with a short meditation.

1 Sit on the floor with knees bent and soles of your feet pressed together so you're in a 'frog' position. Hold the soles of your feet together with both hands.

2 Sit up, so your back is straight, and pull your tummy muscles in towards your spine.

3 Using the muscles in your inner thighs, push your knees down towards the floor. Make sure you don't bounce your knees.

4 When you've got your knees as far as you can go, hold the stretch for ten seconds. Slowly release, then hold for two more sets of 10 seconds.

WATCH POINT
Make sure you don't curl your back. It makes it easier to reach the floor, but you'll be making the stretch less effective.

Hip flexor stretch

This stretch targets the hip flexors (the iliopsoas muscles) as well as the muscles at the front of the thighs. It may feel like a small movement but it has great results. It works really well at easing away the tension in the muscles that may have built up if you've been sitting down for most of the day.

1 Stand with feet hip-width apart and hands resting on your waist.

2 Extend your right leg directly out behind you by about 30 cm (12 inches). Keep both feet flat on the floor.

3 Bend both knees so your whole body drops down towards the floor by 5 cm (2 inches).

4 Letting your heel naturally lift off the floor, tilt your pelvis forwards, bringing your bottom forwards and your hips up. You should immediately feel the stretch in the hip and down the front of the thigh of the extended leg.

5 Hold the stretch for around seven seconds, gently release then hold for another 7 seconds. Repeat with the left leg.

WATCH POINT
You can stay close to a wall or a chair in case you need support.

2

4

2

Quadriceps stretch

The quadriceps muscles are found at the front of your thighs and are often referred to as the 'quads'. Depending on how flexible you are, this stretch may feel quite hard to do at first but it quickly becomes easier. If, on the other hand, you need to feel a bigger stretch, simply thrust slightly forwards the hip of the leg you are stretching.

1 Stand at a right angle to the back of a chair and hold the back with your left hand for support.

2 Keeping your knees together, bend your right leg backwards, grab your right foot or ankle with your right hand, and bring your heel towards your bottom. Make sure you keep your left leg straight, with the knee soft (not locked) and your left foot flat on the floor.

3 Hold the stretch for around 7 seconds, slowly release, then hold for another 7 seconds. Repeat with the left leg.

FOR THE THIGHS

Touch the floor

This stretch targets all the tendons and muscles at the backs of your legs, including the hamstrings and the calves. You should start practising this stretch with legs quite wide apart and, as you get more supple, bring them closer together.

1 Stand with feet slightly more than hip-width apart and arms resting by your sides.

2 Slowly bend over from the waist and reach down to touch the floor. If you can't reach the floor just go as far as you can.

3 Hold the stretch for three sets of 10 seconds, returning to the start position in-between. Do not bounce.

WATCH POINT
Remember to let your head and neck relax – it's tempting to look out in front of you but this will only increase your chances of pulling a muscle in your neck.

Deep lunge

Holding your body in a deep lunge position will really help to stretch out the quads in the extended leg. The deep lunge is commonly used as part of yoga routines, and if you continue to breathe deeply throughout the stretch, you'll find it really relaxing too.

1 Stand with feet 15 cm (6 inches) apart with your hands resting on your hips.

2 Lunge forwards with your right leg so your right knee is bent and your leg is at a right angle to the floor. Make sure your knee doesn't travel beyond your toe. Your right foot should be flat on the floor.

3 Lean forwards and place your hands either side of your right foot. Your left leg should be stretched out behind you with the ball of your foot balancing on the floor.

4 Hold for two sets of 7 seconds on your right leg, returning to the start position in-between, and then repeat with the left leg.

WATCH POINT
Keep your extended leg straight at all times so your knee doesn't touch the floor. This will help make the stretch as beneficial as possible.

2

3

Piriformis stretch

The piriformis muscles lie deep in the gluteal muscles (the ones in your bottom). This is a good stretch to rejuvenate your backside after a long night's sleep.

1 Lie on the floor on your back with both your knees bent, your feet flat on the floor, and palms down by your sides.

2 Lift your right leg off the ground and, rotating your leg from the hip, cross it over so the ankle of your right foot rests just above your left knee. Your right knee should be pointing to the right.

3 Grasp your left thigh with both hands and gently pull your left leg off the floor towards your chest. You will feel the stretch in the outside of your right leg.

4 Hold for two sets of 7 seconds on your right leg and then repeat with the left leg.

WATCH POINT
Make sure you are relaxed all the way through the exercise so that you don't end up locking your hip, and your shoulders remain tension-free.

Seated gluteal stretch

This is a great way to stretch out the muscles in your bottom, while sitting on it! It's quite a hard move to perfect, but the deep, intense stretch will give great results.

1 Sit on the floor with your back straight to create a good posture.

2 Extend your right leg straight out in front of you, keeping your foot flexed.

3 Bend the knee of your left leg and bring it towards you so your left foot is flat on the floor.

4 Cross your left foot over your right leg, so your left foot is level with your right knee.

5 Take your right arm and hug your left knee. Pull it towards your right shoulder until you feel the stretch. Your body should be twisted from the waist. Look to the left.

6 Hold for two sets of 7 seconds, and then repeat with the other leg.

WATCH POINT
If you want to get the best stretch you can, don't lean back. Keep your back straight and the stretch will be more effective.

4

5

Cross and dip

This stretch targets the same muscles as the Seated gluteal stretch, but it will also develop your balance. The stretch will get easier as your calves become more flexible, because you'll be able to lower yourself down further without letting your foot rise up off the floor.

1 Stand behind a chair at a right-angle to it with feet hip-width apart and knees soft. Hold on to the back of the chair with your left hand for support.

2 Bend your right leg and bring your right foot across to meet your left leg, so it's resting above your left knee.

3 Slowly bend the knee of your left leg and lower yourself down towards the floor. Your left foot should remain flat on the floor at all times.

4 As you go down, your left knee should push your right foot higher into the air, which is when you should start to feel the stretch in your right hip, buttock and top of thigh.

5 Once you've gone down as far as you can, hold the stretch for two sets of 7 seconds. Repeat with the other leg.

WATCH POINT
Keep your back straight at all times;
it will stop you from getting a bad back.

Bend and stretch

This is a tried and tested stretch that targets all the muscles at the back of the thighs and in the bottom. Look forwards towards the toes of your extended leg while you are doing the stretch, because it will inspire you to go as far as you can.

1 Stand a large step away from the front of a chair, with feet hip-width apart.

2 Lift your right leg and rest your right foot firmly on the seat of the chair. Your hands should be on your hips.

3 Bend over from the waist, and reach out to touch the toes of your right foot with both hands. You should feel the stretch in your right buttock and thigh.

4 Hold for two sets of 7 seconds on your right leg, without bouncing, and then repeat with the left leg.

WATCH POINT
Make sure that the chair is in the right position – you don't want the foot of your extended leg to be dangling off the edge.

2

3

Runner's calf stretch

As the name suggests, if you do a lot of running or walking you may find that your calves feel tight and inflexible. This stretch will help them feel loose and tension-free.

1 Get down on the floor on your hands and knees, with your knees resting directly below your hips and your hands below your shoulders. Curl your toes under so they are resting on the floor.

2 Push up off the floor with both hands and straighten your legs, pushing your bottom into the air. Your elbows and knees should be soft.

1

3 Try to lower your heels gently to the floor. Hold for three sets of 10 seconds, returning to the start position in-between.

WATCH POINT
This is quite a difficult stretch and you may not be able to hold it for the full 10 seconds at first. Just try your best and don't give up.

2

Push-off calf stretch

You usually see joggers doing this stretch before a big run – that's because it's a really good way of performing a controlled calf stretch that targets the gastrocnemius muscle (the big muscle at the back of the calf). To get the best stretch possible, make sure your full weight is shifted towards the wall.

1 Stand at arm's length from the wall, with your feet shoulder-width apart.

2 Extend your right leg out in front of you and bend your right knee.

3 Place the palms of your hands, at shoulder height, flat against the wall.

4 Take one step back with your left leg and, keeping it straight, press your heel firmly into the floor. You should feel the stretch in the calf of your left leg. Keep your hips facing the wall and your rear leg and spine in a straight line.

5 Hold the stretch for two sets of 7 seconds, then repeat with the other leg.

WATCH POINT
If you want to feel a greater stretch, simply move your extended leg a little bit further away from the wall.

4

2

CALVES & ANKLES

3

Soleus stretch

The soleus muscle is a small muscle in the calf, which is situated slightly lower down in the leg, under the gastrocnemius. It's usually quite hard to target, but this stretch will give it a good once-over.

1 Stand in front of a wall with feet shoulder-width apart and flat on the floor.

2 Bend your knees and drop your buttocks down towards the floor a short way.

3 Place your palms flat against the wall and gently lean towards the wall until you feel the stretch in your lower calf muscles. Hold for three sets of 10 seconds.

WATCH POINT

This is a more subtle stretch than those that target the gastrocnemius muscles. If you're finding it hard to feel the stretch, simply step back a bit from the wall and bend your knees a little bit more.

Point and flex stretch

This is a really easy stretch to do and it may remind you of having dance classes as a child. It's best to keep doing the movement explained below rather than holding the stretch for a set period of time. Make sure you put the effort into really pointing and flexing the feet – the further you go, the better the stretch.

1 Sit on the floor with both legs stretched out in front of you. Sit upright with your back straight and your hands resting on the floor by your bottom for support.

2 Start by flexing your feet towards you as far as you can get them. Then, point them away from you down to the floor as far as you can.

3 Keep repeating the movement slowly until the 30 seconds are up.

WATCH POINT
Try not to rush the movement. Your priority is to feel the stretch rather than do as many repetitions as you can in the time allowed.

2

2

Push down

The Push down is a great warm-up for the stomach and waist. It's a really gentle movement that helps to get you warm, while stretching out your major muscles.

1 Stand with feet hip-width apart and your hands resting by your sides. Make sure your legs are straight with knees soft.

2 Lean to the right, sliding your right arm down your right thigh towards your knee as you go. Keep your back straight and your head and neck in line with your spine at all times. You should feel the stretch in your left side.

3 Hold for two sets of seven seconds, returning to the starting position in-between, then repeat on your left side.

WATCH POINT
You don't need to tilt over very far, just aim to touch the side of your knee with your hand.

Up and over

This exercise is an old-style way of targeting the muscles at the side of your waist, which are called the obliques. It's a great way of stretching out your love handles and it also helps you to feel really refreshed in the morning.

1 Stand with feet hip-width apart and your hands resting by your sides. Make sure your legs are slightly bent with knees soft. Keep your back straight and your head and neck in line with your spine.

2 Raise your left arm over your head and lean over from the waist to the right, so that your right hand travels down the side of your right leg. Your left arm should be reaching up and over your head. You should feel the stretch in the left side of your waist.

3 Hold for two sets of 7 seconds then slowly return to the starting position and repeat on the other side.

WATCH POINT
Don't try to stretch down too far —
just do enough to feel it working.

Oblique stretch

This is an easy way to give the muscles in your waist a really good stretch. As you walk your hands around to get into position, you may not be able to reach your knees but that's fine – just go as far round as you can comfortably.

1 Get down on the floor on all fours with your knees resting directly below your hips and your hands below your shoulders.

2 Keeping your knees where they are, walk both your hands around to your right-hand side to meet your knees, so you are twisting from the waist. You should feel the stretch down your left-hand side. Hold the stretch for 10 seconds then walk the hands back round to the starting position.

3 Repeat the movement so you are stretching round to the left-hand side.

1

2

WATCH POINT
Pull your tummy muscles in while you do this exercise – it will help to stop your back from arching.

Hip mobilization

You'll feel this stretch across your tummy, as you circle your hips around. It's also a great way of loosening up your hips, so it's a good stretch for starting the day.

1 Stand with feet slightly further than hip-width apart.

2 Rest your hands on your waist and begin by slowly rotating your hips clockwise in a circular motion. Make sure you are in control of the movement and your legs stay slightly bent with feet firmly on the ground. To get the movement right, keep your back straight and try not to stick your bottom out.

3 After 15 seconds, repeat the same movement but this time in an anticlockwise direction.

WATCH POINT
You should be rotating from the hips, which, when done correctly, shouldn't cause your back to arch or give you any pain. Practise this one before you start the routine – you'll be able to tell when you're doing it right by the way it feels.

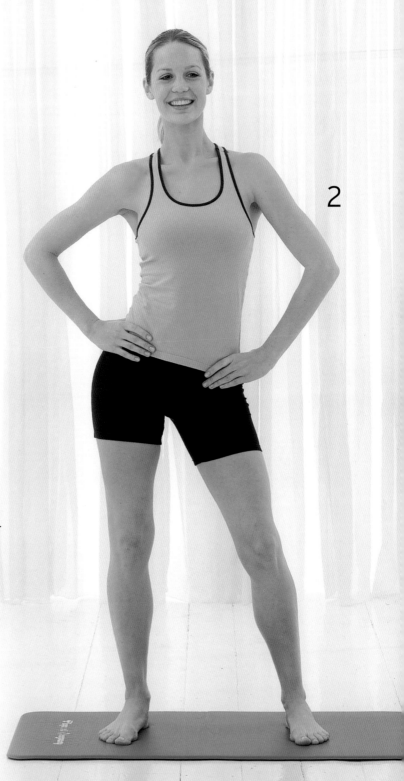

2

Easy chest stretch

This stretch targets the pectoral muscles, sometimes known as the 'pecs', which are the major muscles at the front of the chest. It will also give your supraspinatus muscle, which runs along the top of your shoulder blades, a nice big stretch.

1 You can either stand with feet hip-width apart, or you can do this stretch while sitting on a chair. Whichever position you prefer, make sure that your back is straight and your head and neck are in line with your spine.

2 Bring your arms up to shoulder level and bend from the elbows so that your hands are hovering in front of your chest. Make loose fists with your hands.

3 Leading from the elbow, gently rotate both arms backwards so that you're squeezing your shoulder blades together. Your chest will automatically push out a little.

4 Hold for 10 seconds then release. Repeat this three times.

WATCH POINT
It's quite easy to get tired while doing this stretch but, if you persevere, you will get great results.

Front-lying chest lift

The Front-lying chest lift is usually used as part of a yoga pose. It's great for stretching out all the muscles across the chest, including the pecs.

1 Lie face-down on the floor with your palms on the floor either side of your chest.

2 Keeping your hips and thighs on the floor, push up with your hands and arms so that your chest is off the floor. Don't come up too far – aim to lift your chest just a short distance off the floor.

3 Hold the pose for 10 seconds then release and return to the starting position. Repeat twice more.

WATCH POINT
Some of you may find it hard to arch the back as you lift yourself up into the pose – it depends how flexible you already are. If you can't lift your chest far off the floor, don't abandon this stretch – it will get easier with time.

2

Shoulder stretch

This is an easy stretch to do, and will really get your shoulders loosened up. It's great to do if you've been particularly stressed-out recently, because it will help to get rid of any built-up tension.

1 You can do this stretch from either a standing or a seated position. Extend your right arm directly out in front of you so it's parallel with the floor.

2 Using your left hand, grip the back of your right arm between your elbow and your shoulder and use it to bring your right arm gently across the front of your chest. You should feel the stretch down the inner side of your right arm and across your right shoulder blade.

3 Hold the position for two sets of 7 seconds and then repeat with the other arm.

WATCH POINT
Stop yourself from rotating by making sure your hips are facing forwards at all times.

Pec stretch

Your pectoral muscles (pecs) are the
big muscles that sit under your bust.
Stretching them out will help get rid
of any knots or tension that may have
built up from carrying heavy bags. Plus,
this stretch will help encourage deep
breathing, which will enable you to feel
a whole lot perkier and more refreshed
in the morning.

1 Stand with feet hip-width apart.
Place your palms on your lower back
then gently pull your shoulders back
together and stick your chest out until you
feel the stretch. Keep your elbows soft.

2 Hold the stretch for three sets of
10 seconds.

WATCH POINT
When you bring your shoulders back, be careful not
to arch your back. All the movement should come
from the shoulders.

1

Inner arm stretch

This targets all the muscles in your upper arms – you'll be surprised at how easy it is to feel the stretch.

1 Stand in an open door frame, with your abs tight and body straight.

2 Hold on to the door frame with your left hand just below shoulder level, or as high as is comfortable. Take a big step forwards so your left arm is extended out behind you. Keeping your hips facing forwards and your head and neck in line with your spine, rotate your upper body to the right until you feel the stretch in your left arm. Lean forwards to feel a greater stretch.

3 Hold for two sets of 7 seconds then turn around, step forwards and repeat the stretch with your right arm.

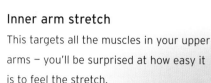

2

WATCH POINT
Don't worry if you find it difficult to get your arm up to shoulder height because you can still achieve a good stretch by having it slightly lower.

Bicep stretch

The bicep muscles are the big muscles at the front of your upper arms. It's good to stretch them out so you develop long, lean arms that look great in sleeveless tops!

1 Stand with feet hip-width apart, stomach muscles pulled in and hands resting by your sides.

2 Extend your right arm out in front of you with your palm flat, facing the ceiling.

3 Extend your left arm, placing the left palm on top of the right palm. Gently push your hands against each other. You will feel the stretch in your biceps.

4 Hold for three sets of 10 seconds, then repeat for the other arm.

WATCH POINT
Don't try to force your hands together with a lot of pressure. Just take it slowly and start with a small amount of pressure in order to achieve a gentle stretch.

4

3

Tricep stretch

Your tricep muscles are found at the back of the top of your arms. Giving them a good stretch will boost circulation and help to get rid of any blotchy, pimply skin that may reside there.

1 Stand with feet hip-width apart. Lift your right arm above your head and bend your elbow so your hand drops down behind your neck.

2 Grip your right elbow with your left hand and pull it gently to the left – this will automatically force your right hand to dip down between your shoulder blades. You should feel the tricep muscle stretch in your right arm. Keep your chin lifted, so you don't put a strain on your neck.

3 Hold the stretch for two sets of 7 seconds then repeat the stretch, working your left arm instead.

WATCH POINT

This movement makes it really easy to let your head fall forwards so your chin is resting on your chest, but don't let this happen because it will put a strain on your neck. Keep your chin lifted and eyes forward throughout the stretch.

Seashell stretch

This stretch is great at targeting the muscles in your shoulders as well as your back. Just sit back and relax and you will feel the beneficial effects of the stretch.

1 Get down on the floor on your hands and knees. Sit back on to your calves, so your bottom is resting on your heels. Make sure your neck and head are relaxed and that you are looking down towards the floor.

2 Stretch your arms out in front of you so that your hands and fingertips are spread on the floor.

3 Walk your hands as far forwards as you can until you can feel the stretch in the middle of your back.

4 Hold the stretch for three sets of 10 seconds.

WATCH POINT
Don't strain your neck by trying to look in front of you – it's best to let your head and neck relax so you are looking down towards the floor.

1

3

Upper back stretch

Stretching out the muscles in the back will have a therapeutic effect on both your body and your state of mind. The back is one of the first areas to retain tension and stress, so stretching out the muscles will help to put you at ease and set you up for the day ahead.

1 Stand with feet hip-width apart.

2 Interlink your fingers and push your hands out in front of you as far as possible. Your palms should be facing away from you.

3 Allow your upper back to relax by lowering your shoulders to their natural resting position.

4 Hold for 10 seconds. You should feel the stretch between your shoulder blades. Pause for a brief moment, then repeat the stretch twice more.

WATCH POINT

If you find it hard to get your back to relax, just take a deep breath and lower your shoulders. This will have an instant relaxing effect.

3

Knee squeezes

The Knee squeeze is a subtle way of stretching out the muscles across the middle of your back. This stretch feels very satisfying when done correctly, so spend some time making sure you get it right.

1 Lie on the floor with your knees bent and feet flat on the floor. Let your arms rest by your sides.

2 Gently bring your knees back towards your chest.

3 Engage your stomach muscles by pulling them in towards your spine and lift your tailbone ever so slightly off the floor. Grip your knees with your hands for support. You should feel a stretch across the middle of your back.

4 Hold the stretch for three sets of 10 seconds, taking a very brief pause in-between.

WATCH POINT
It's common to want to hold your breath during this stretch but make sure you don't. Breathe slowly and deeply and you will make the stretch easier to do and more effective.

Lower back stretch

This stretch is ideal for targeting the muscles across your lower back, which have a tendency to ache, especially if you've had a bad night's sleep. Stretching them in the morning will help to reduce your risk of injury during the day.

3

1 Stand with feet hip-width apart and knees slightly bent.

2 Place your hands on your inner thighs with your palms facing outwards.

3 Engage your abdominals and slowly arch your spine until you feel a stretch across your lower back.

4 Hold for around 8 seconds then slowly stretch up through the spine until you are back in a normal standing position. Keep your back straight, with your chin up and looking forwards.

5 Repeat the stretch three times.

WATCH POINT
If you're not feeling the stretch, simply move your palms further down your thighs – this should help to increase it.

Waist and lower spine

This is another great way of targeting your lower back muscles and really stretching them out. If you do it slowly and gently, it can even be good at soothing lower back problems.

2

1 Lie on the floor on your back with your legs straight out and your right arm extended out to the side.

2 Bending your right leg, grip your knee with your left hand and bring it over to your left-hand side so it gets as close to the floor as is comfortable. Keep your right hand extended out to your right-hand side because this will help to increase the stretch in your waist and lower spine.

3 Hold the stretch for two sets of 7 seconds with a brief pause between. Repeat on your right side.

WATCH POINT
When you are stretching to the left side, make sure you keep the right hip on the floor and vice versa. This will stop you from stretching too far over and putting a strain on your lower back.

Cat stretch

This stretch is known as the Cat stretch because you look a lot like a cat if you do it right! It targets most of the major muscles in the back.

1 Get down on the floor on all fours. Let your head and neck relax so they are in line with your spine and you are looking down towards the floor.

2 Slowly arch your back, by pulling in your tummy muscles and pushing the curve of your spine towards the ceiling. Tilt your head and neck up towards the ceiling as you do this.

3 Hold the stretch for around 8 seconds then lower your back so it's straight and in the starting position again. While you do this, let your head and neck relax also.

4 Pause for a brief moment then repeat three times.

5 When you have finished, lean back on to your heels and stretch your arms out in front of you – this completes the movement.

WATCH POINT
Try not to let your back sag because this could cause serious back injuries. You can avoid this by doing the stretch slowly and gently to make sure you are in control at all times.

2

5

Neck stretches

This is a great substitute for a neck massage. It really helps to get your muscles loose, warm and nicely stretched. Plus, it's much safer than rolling your neck, because it puts less of a strain on the surrounding muscles.

1 Stand up straight with feet hip-width apart. Relax your shoulders and look straight ahead of you.

2 Start the stretch by slowly lowering your chin to your chest. Hold for a few seconds while you feel the stretch across the back of your neck and then gently raise your head so it's back in the starting position.

3 Next, rotate your head to the right and hold for a few seconds, then rotate your head to the left. Hold for a few seconds then return to the start position so you are looking straight ahead.

4 Repeat the sequence three times, until the 30 seconds are up.

WATCH POINT
Make sure your hips are facing forwards at all times – it's just your head that's supposed to be rotating, not your entire body!

2

3

3

This two-week plan is an example of the way you can structure your stretching regime. We've chosen a mixture of different stretches to target each of the major muscle groups in the body to give you a great all-over programme.

You'll do two sets of six stretches each morning to last for 6 minutes. If you want to draw up your own plan you can. However, we recommend you start with our plan and monitor your results – how flexible you become and how relaxed you feel – then you can adapt it if you need to. Now, let's get started...

Day 1

Seated hamstring stretch p10
Piriformis stretch p16
Runner's calf stretch p20
Push down p24
Easy chest stretch p30
Upper back stretch p38

Day 2

Inner thigh stretch p11
Seated gluteal stretch p17
Push-off calf stretch p21
Up and over p25
Front-lying chest lift p31
Knee squeezes p39

Day 3

Day 5

Day 4

Day 6

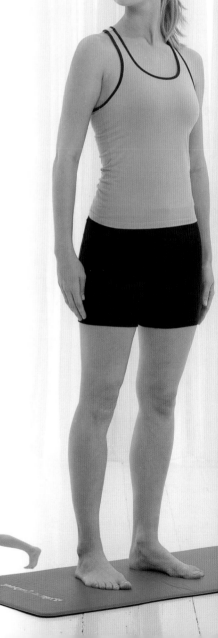

Day 7

Seated hamstring stretch **p10**

Bend and stretch **p19**

Soleus stretch **p22**

Push down **p24**

Tricep stretch **p36**

Neck stretches **p43**

Day 9

Hip flexor stretch **p12**

Seated gluteal stretch **p17**

Soleus stretch **p22**

Twist **p26**

Seashell stretch **p37**

Knee squeezes **p39**

Day 8

Inner thigh stretch **p11**

Piriformis stretch **p16**

Point and flex stretch **p23**

Up and over **p25**

Easy chest stretch **p30**

Upper back stretch **p38**

Day 10

Quadriceps stretch **p13**

Cross and dip **p18**

Runner's calf stretch **p20**

Full body stretch **p27**

Front-lying chest lift **p31**

Lower back stretch **p40**

Day 11

Touch the floor **p14**
Bend and stretch **p19**
Push-off calf stretch **p21**
Oblique stretch **p28**
Easy chest stretch **p30**
Inner arm stretch **p34**

Day 13

Inner thigh stretch **p11**
Seated gluteal stretch **p17**
Point and flex stretch **p23**
Push down **p24**
Inner arm stretch **p34**
Cat stretch **p42**

Day 12

Deep lunge **p15**
Piriformis stretch **p16**
Soleus stretch **p22**
Hip mobilization **p29**
Shoulder stretch **p32**
Waist and lower spine **p41**

Day 14

Quadriceps stretch **p13**
Cross and dip **p18**
Runner's calf stretch **p20**
Up and over **p25**
Tricep stretch **p36**
Lower back stretch **p40**

INDEX